Titanium CV

Sharpening Resume
For Tougher Job Market

By Lee Peng Yeow

Titanium CV

Sharpening Resume
For Tougher Job Market

Published by Lee Peng Yeow

First Published 2010

ISBN: 978-981-05-9028-4

DEDICATION

This book is dedicated to my lovely wife Flossie Poh Po Lay and my dearest son Lee Joe Ray. Love you all!

Special thanks to friends who have contributed their resumes for illustrations. They have trusted me to sharpen their resumes. My effort is little but our friendship is TITANIUM!

Titanium CV

PREFACE

Job Seekers and the Employed

In today employment world, Job Seekers and the Employed face many dilemmas: globalization, economies restructuring, financial meltdown etc. are not within our control. People gets retrenched or laid off by companies who did or did not do well enough. Even if you are employed now, you fear that you will lose your job someday to cheaper labor whether foreign and domestic. Not forgetting that innovation could replace labor altogether. Further aggregating the facets, our age will catch up over time and existing skill may be something of the past. Amidst all these happenings, people still need a continuous income to sustain living. Everyone wants to get out of this cycle by looking for a better employment but competition in the labor market is sure tough. People have shared with me that they sent hundreds of job application and received only a few responses; if not none. If all things begin equal and that getting a job interview is crucial to show and tell your prospective employer that you can do a better job, you will need to start somewhere.

This book is written for aspiring individual whose expertise are not telecast deep enough to get your prospective employers' attention. This is probably the reason why you are not frequently called up for job interview. The culprit could just be your CV (CV=Curriculum Vitae)!

Over many years of manpower recruiting, I have seen many poorly written resumes and few good ones. But let me clarify: many candidates are good in English but they did poorly to "market" themselves. "Marketing" and "Up-selling" yourself are not uncommon buzz words that appear popularly in many resume-writing books today. Candidates had self-acclaimed that they are highly marketable but the resumes were neither impressive nor the actual turn-out during the interview. In a tight market where hiring manager needs to pick the right candidate among large pool of job applicants, "marketing" one-self has to be quickly-made visible, fact-based and very recitative in your head. When the fact-based "marketing" stuff is translated onto the resume in some logical fashion, it must stand out to the hiring manager who read your resume. By "some logical fashion", I mean the hiring manager's "fashion", not yours.

To tell you that Titanium CV will land you on your ideal job is definitely a lie. The outcome of Titanium CV is neither about if you get your ideal job nor the number of jobs offers. It success is more measurable by how many interviews you get to go after you release your rejuvenated version. Statistics have proven that there is a far large improvement; provided that you get your resume rejuvenated right for the job you applied. Well-written Cover Letter has proven for Human Resources to call candidate within hours after the cover letter was sent through electronic mailing.

Job Market

Job market is more volatile today than before for 2 reasons. One, companies across industries have to adjust constantly to align with the changing business landscapes.

Changing businesses requires constantly feeding of new breed of skilled workers and talents at a sustainable cost structure. The human resource division in any organization is force to look at innovative means to hire right and the most efficient way to spend manpower's dollar.

Unlike the old industry that requires a professional to stay in a specific field, the new economy requires a professional to behave in multi-dimension manner. Here is a list of new behaviors that will not surprise many job seekers and the Employed:

- Multiple verses Single roles
- Proactive verses Passive or Reactive working behavior
- Embrace responsibilities verses waiting for job dedication from the Superior
- See contract placement as permanent placement
- Entrepreneur-rat seeking cheese verses conventional rat racing
- Outsourcing is a norm

The contemporary behaviors tell us that we need to re-write our resume in a way that speaks your prospective employer's language.

HOW THIS BOOK IS ORGANISED ?

Major Book Sections	Job Seeker's Metaphor	Hiring Expectations	Resume Sharpening	Additional Readings
Objectives	A key component to normalize mindset about job seeking today.	Show you why and what you need to drive your resume towards hiring expectations on a hiring manager's position plan.	A suite of sharpening techniques that improves a resume appeal and in turn, improves your marketability. Get your resume ready, sharpen it according to the techniques taught and apply job immediately.	The author tells you how hiring manager can call you for interview; sometimes even without reading your resume. A broad base career map is introduced using the tool: Career Pyramid. A short peep into how fresh graduates could have written their resumes.
Location	Chapter 1 - 2	Chapter 3	Chapter 4 - 10	Chapter 11 - 13

About this Book

The book is organized into 3 major blocks: Job Seekers' Metaphor, Hiring Expectations and Resume Sharpening. The illustration shows the major blocks and brief rundowns of the key objectives for each block.

The key take-away from the book:

(i)   **Job Seeker's Metaphor**
        We beginning by cracking the myths of resume to tell you that resume is not your fairytale for someone else but a concrete brick-and-mortar foundation, laid down layer by layer to tell your own story.

        Before you even begin to pen down anything, you begin my identifying your "distinction". This will set you thinking real hard of what sets you apart from others. Thinking it is so simple, you begin by drawing a self analogy about Strength and Weakness. That where most people get it wrong! Those are the standards! It won't cut you from the rest!

We introduce another essential metaphor: Make Everyday Your Learning Day. That sound like another easy one! This won't do you any good if every day is a chore to you, repetitive and becomes habitual. You need to trigger the mind to learn a thing or two every day.

New traits like business acumen, cross-culture behaviors etc. are emerging in candidate's personality profiling. Employers expect job applicants to bear one or more of these traits. Are you ready for these traits or answer questions relating to these traits? You may not be comfortable with the traits but are you willing to take up the challenges if you really win the job?

(ii) **Hiring Expectations**

Hiring managers have very little time to screen through each and every resumes and therefore, we focus on writings that appeal to hiring managers. This is crucial in planning "what to write" and "how to write" a resume.

(iii)   Resume Sharpening

Powerful writing techniques that enhance and add-value to your resume will be discussed here. Do not expect to find ton of resumes' samples in the book because quantity samples do not improve the quality of resume writing. Rejuvenation writing techniques are demonstrated in several parts of a sample resume so that you get very focus on the details to pick, polish and re-present it. However, that does not mean that one technique used in one part of the resume cannot be used elsewhere. Good resume writer uses various techniques in many parts of the resume and even in cover letter. An entire chapter is dedicated to tell you what good cover letter is all about.

This book is different from the usual resume-writing books in many ways. I teach my students how to strengthen their resumes, not how to write resumes. When you have grabbed the techniques and applied them consciously in writing, you no longer need this book anymore.

Please help to pass it on to someone who may need it!

Lee Peng Yeow

Titanium CV

TABLE OF CONTENT

JOB SEEKER'S METAPHOR

CHAPTER 1

THE MYTHS OF RESUME

If there are myths just about anything on earth, there are myths associated with a resume. To write an "up selling" and "magnetic" resume, start with a walk-through on common myths about resume.

Like my younger days, many job seekers have unconsciously accepted the 7 myths about resume. The myths prevent us from finding new means to write better resume. As I unfold the myths, ask yourself if you have ever been "locked-up" by them innocently.

Re-Thinking the Myths
Let begin by flashing the myths' cards.

MYTH 1

I start to write my resume when I am about to join the work force because I need a resume to apply for jobs.

MYTH 2

Once a job is found, I sweep my resume aside to collect dust until I need to find the next job.

MYTH 3

The next time I update my resume, I top it up with the experience in my current job....

MYTH 4

My resume is written for someone else i.e. for the hiring manager, not for myself.

MYTH 5

Resume should be humbly written. My competence will automatically surface on the resume to the hiring manager who read it.

MYTH 6

I will leave the self-selling till the day of the face-to-face interview.

MYTH 7

Resume is strictly "For-Your-Eyes-Only". I do not normally share my resume with my colleagues, friends etc.

Without disputing the myths, you can carry these myths with you like a second nature.

Disputing the Myths

If you have been accepting the myths, a resume is none other than a few pieces of papers that describe about you for someone else. Ask yourself if you are worth a few pieces of papers? Nobody has taught us to re-look at our resume and so, should we? Shouldn't we just reverse what the myths imply and see if you can find some breakthroughs?

The rest of this section will reveal the cornerstone of myths and not the stepping stone, of successful resume writing.

(a) **Prepare Resume in Your Early Days**

You need to write your resume as early as your college days, if not, sooner! You may ask why? Simple things like running errands for your school's football team demonstrate your commitment and how you conduct yourself towards attaining them. Therefore, resume writing does not necessary begin only when you step out into the working life. Without real job experience, you can still sell your good personal attributes and contributions in your school days.

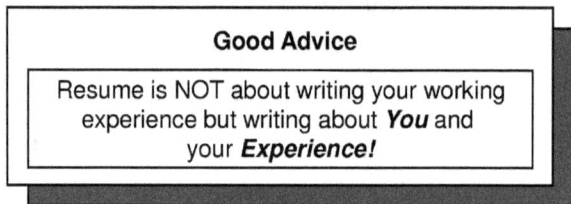

Good Advice

Resume is NOT about writing your working experience but writing about *You* and your *Experience!*

Fig 1.1 Good Advice No. 1

(b)   Update Your Resume Every 6 Months

You may not have changed your job but you must have learned something new on the same job for the last 6 months.

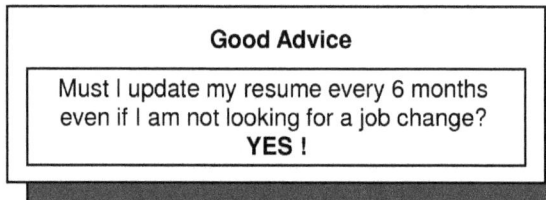

Good Advice

Must I update my resume every 6 months even if I am not looking for a job change?
YES !

Fig 1.2 Good Advice No. 2

If I challenge you to an exercise: for the next 10 minutes, write down your top 10 achievements for the last 6 months, are you able to do so?

Most people fail this test. They find it so hard to write down their top 10 achievement for the last 6 months. Most people do have achievements but they just cannot recall them. Try recalling your achievements for the last 2 years?

(c) **Not Good Enough To Update Your Resume Only With Current Working Experience**

It is common that seasoned job seekers transit in and out of different jobs. These job seekers describe the different jobs diligently into the resume in a chronological order. But one tiny thing is missing here: the correlation of the different jobs.

Say, if you went through two very different jobs, as long as you cannot correlates the jobs in a progressive fashion; you will lose the "mission" in your career progression. Therefore, how you present your career transition is imperative. I have heard how candidates explained this: change of professions, prefer to work in another line, change of environment etc. These are definitely not the best ways you can explain them.

Employer prefers candidate who have a clear, holistic approach in their career pursuit. Your resume can become easier to "fish" when prospective employer looks for evidences to group work history together and attempt to assess if they are good enough to fulfill the job requirement. If you do this on your resume deliberately, isn't it far easier for the prospective employer to understand how you have transit in your career wisely?

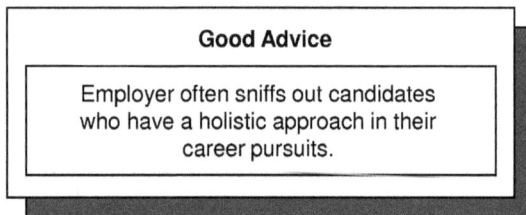

Good Advice

Employer often sniffs out candidates who have a holistic approach in their career pursuits.

Fig 1.3 Good Advice No. 3

(d) **Do Not Leave Self-Selling Till the Interview Day**

Each time a company advertises a job position, the hiring manager will screen through lots of resumes from the applicants. If your resume fails to catch his attention, you may not even have an opportunity to be called up for an interview.

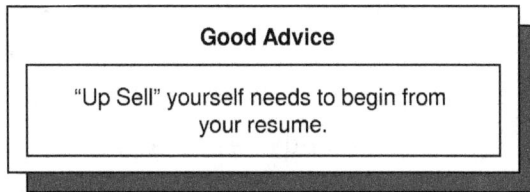

Good Advice

"Up Sell" yourself needs to begin from your resume.

Fig 1.4 Good Advice No. 4

(e) **Resume Is Not "For-Your-Eyes-Only"**

Most people treats resume as confidential and only "authorized" people can view it. People are generally reluctant to show their resumes to their friends and colleagues.

Ask the same group of people this question: When you drop your resume with a hiring agency, who do you think will be reading your resume? The hiring agency is a total stranger to you and yet you prefer to share your resume with a stranger than to share it with someone you probably already know for ages?

With the convenience of Internet, hiring agencies get on the Internet and invite you to drop your resume with them for a job hunt. Ton of people uploaded their resumes without even knowing the people at the other end....or is there somebody really at the other end? Hiring agency often assured you that all resumes are treated with "Strict Confident" ....hmm... let's not doubt about professionalism and industry integrity here!

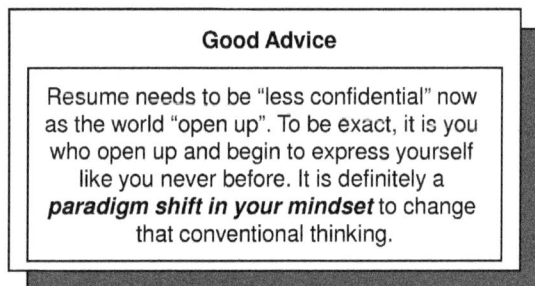

Good Advice

Resume needs to be "less confidential" now as the world "open up". To be exact, it is you who open up and begin to express yourself like you never before. It is definitely a **paradigm shift in your mindset** to change that conventional thinking.

Fig 1.5 Good Advice No. 5

The acid test that I used to challenge my students if they are mentally-ready to "market" themselves using their resumes is this:

In a class of slightly more than 10 students, I told them to swap their resumes with the person sitting next to him or her. Over 80% of the students were dumb-founded. These students were hesitating if they should be exchanging their resumes even thought before this, I asked and every student claimed that they understood they need to "marketing themselves to the world".

Should Confidential Information Be Included in the Resume?

One student argued on the fact that the resume will carry very personal information, for example, the past salaries. Exchanging resumes in the class especially with your peer can be a potential risk of leaking P&C (Private and Confidential) information.

Remember, all marketing brochures sell features and benefits. The only reason you stated the price on a market brochure is the time you want to tell the public you have a price advantage over competitors and it make absolute sense to buyers and consumers. If this is the case, what is stopping you to put the "past salaries" on the resume and telling the world that you are cheaper and better (if this is going to be your marketing tag line).

The so-called personal and confidential information, it really up to you. But if you knew specific information is "confidential", will you still publish openly?

If you are ready, adopt an open approach to resume writing. Resume is something you want the world to know you better. The world out there is always fearful especially you are about to share personal information. I only need you to tell the world something interesting about you and your career.

CHAPTER 2
MINDSET

Generally, in the course of our life, you might have done a SWOT (Strengths, Weakness, Opportunities and Threats) assessment on your personalities and behaviors. You probably got some ready answers when you are probed on your strengths or weaknesses during a job interview. The tricky part about the Strength is the flip side: the Weakness. Deliberately, when you think of Strength, you try not to collide with Weakness. Otherwise, it gets very embarrassing when the interviewer found out that your Strength-Weakness ends in a deadlock.

We can try a different approach to uncover our personality. I called this the Distinction Self-Assessment. The objective is to find out what you are so special. Unlike Strength and Weakness, there is no flip side to Distinction.

Distinction Self Assessment
Take the next 5 minutes to ponder on this question:

- What are the things in you that make you distinct? What are they?

Identify Your Distinction

Think about a popular pop star that you adore. What is so "distinct" about this pop star? It is the voice, the music or the performance? You may be attracted to one or many of these distinct attributes. These distinctions explain why the pop star is unique. It is this distinction that you need to identify and write about yourself. This distinction will give you the cutting edge above the candidates who come to compete with you for the job.

Think about your distinction? Often, it is something you do very well. It can be a hobby or professional work that you have achieved a great deal of self satisfaction, recognition from peers or your superior. For examples,

- I am very resourceful in organizing community events
- I am very strong in debugging a software program

- I enjoy convincing people about my product
- I love gardening and know the secret receipt to grow ladies' fingers up to 2 feet long.
- Outside my accounting profession, I have flair in training and coaching in soft skill.
- I have 10 years of retail sales operation.

Supposing you wrote a book to teach people how to make money by doing small businesses. However, before you publish the book, you decide to get 5 people to proof read the book. In return, what you get is a whole lot of criticism about how silly your ideas were to make small businesses. Such criticism may elicit lousy work, unsuccessful attempt and losing-money ideas. But one fact remains unchanged: You can write well. You are unable to conceive a strong business idea because it requires business skill. Your distinction is Writing Skill, not Business Skill.

When you apply your distinction into a job, it does not imply you may be passionate about the job. It just means that you do exceptional well compare with others. Make no mistake. We are not talking about passionate personality or the perfect dream job. But you can be the cream of top of the cake if you are pulling the relevant facts and arrange them well.

Now that you know about Distinction, have you identify your distinction before? Or vaguely you did but it is only on a passing cloud. Did you seriously give it a thought?

Make Everyday A Learning Day

Why did you leave your last job? Whenever this question is brought up during an interview, job applicants' replies fell into five of these popular answers:

- Change of environment
- Move away from office politics
- Expect higher salary
- Expect better prospects
- Learned everything in the current job

Look closely at the last answer. Even you have learned everything in your current job, answering in this manner could do more harm than you thought. Hiring manager prefer candidates to be inspired beyond his/her job scope. They love candidates who seek challenges and treat every day as a day for learning.

As an author, I embrace everyday as a learning day. I may increase my vocabularies today and sharpen my story lines tomorrow and it goes on... so there is never a NO learning day.

But if everyday learning is not a second nature to you now, you need to change it right away. There are more benefits to adopt the habit of everyday learning than to make a harmful statement during the course of an interview.

For those who are keen to pick up the habit, begin learning bit-by-bit a day to make a winning day! Do not under-estimate this small fella: in a year, you get to learn 365 things at the end of the year.

Having said that adopting everyday learning habit is so important, the next question on your mind should be: What am I going to learn? Does it matter to the interviewer?

The truth is this: It is for you to convince the hiring manager that you have an everyday-learning altitude and it does matter that the things you learn continue to build on your distinction.

For examples, "I read Outsourcing magazine and forum as a daily diet to keep me abreast of how things are changing with your businesses"..... A job applicant aiming for a customer services position.

"Though I am out of job for the last 6 months, I enroll myself with the local communities to participate in social activities, create events and educate the younger volunteers to understand about their community works. My mind is even more active now." .... A senior job applicant explaining he is capable of doing a young man's job.

"I network with business people extensively even outside my working hours to gain relationship and friendship; preparing myself for bigger role in marketing and sales." .... A semi-experience marketer tries to win a Marketing Manager position.

Changing Beliefs to Take New Actions

Try answering these questions:

- Who influences you to take a specific bus and travel a specific route to the office? You!

- Who influences you to type a covering letter, attaches a resume and mails the job application out? Again, you!.

- Who influenced you to bottom-up last evening? The drink-till-drunk colleagues? Yes! But you are convinced to hang out with them. It is still you!

Your action is a result of an execution path programmed inside your head. By default, common sense tells us a person has many execution paths or more than one choices. The selected path is a result of conscious decision derived after considering many complex factors.

You may think that it is a complex chain of reasonings to select a specific execution path. But if you have been selecting a particular execution path in response to the same line of reasonings, it quickly becomes a "habit". It follows that if the execution path does not change, the action you take will not change very much.

Our human nature tends to adopt a die-hard, "habitual" belief that becomes too comfortable for us to change it. Even we have wealth of intelligent to choose something else; our habitual belief will prevent us from stretching out of the "comfort" zone.

Job interview questions are designed to understand you and your belief better. This is especially true if hiring manager wants to know if you are prepared to join a company with a different corporate culture. Here are some examples of this form of questions:

- Are you independent but also a team player?
- Can you work with all levels of people?
- Are you cross-culture friendly?

- Do you see customer's feedback as sign of loyalty or attack?
- Are you entrepreneur's savvy?
- Are you able to travel extensively?
- Do you have the business acumen? etc.

Though it may apply only to specific job, companies are looking for one or more of these traits in a job applicant today. Candidate needs a different battle-gear that armed with traits like entrepreneur-savvy, business acumen, team work etc.

But wait! What is really business acumen? My University never taught me that at all! And travel extensively? You mean I need to travel alone and 50% out of country? I worked in a SME company with only 35 people for a whole 3 years. Is this working with all levels of people?

Do you feel any pinch of reluctance to pick up one or more of these new traits for challenges if you win the job?

Mindset That Matters

One different you can see yourself tomorrow from today is the ability to define your distinction, genuinely adopting continuous learning attitude and be prepared to change with new traits. Hiring manager will massage questions in many forms to dig answers from you. Each times your limbo on interviewer questions, you will probably need to go back and revisit this chapter and think through to find answers. There is no perfect answer whether if you are ready. But when you do win a job, it means that you have done some home works; one way or another.

HIRING
EXPECTATIONS

CHAPTER 3
HIRING MANAGER'S TOOLS KIT

The first reason I requested for an interview with a candidate is because I have no clue about this person's interest for the job. A candidate may meet all the selection criteria in the Position Plan but the resume gave me no clue why he is interested for the job. Whenever there is more than one applicant, are you really one cut above?

To differentiate yourself from the herd, I shall teach you how to write a resume away from the old fashion way. In the old fashion way, you write down what you hope the target audience would see. Our new method writes with the target audience in mind as oppose to what you feel should be in a resume. It is the target audience that matters, not you.

For job application, naturally the target audience is the hiring manager. By understanding how the hiring manager filters his candidates, you can be smarter and set your resume right. One common tool used by many hiring manager is *The Position Plan* (commonly known as JD – The Job Description). The hiring manager used it to screen and filter candidate objectively.

Not many people get to see a position plan which is none other than a list of screening criteria. But you as a candidate can use the same position plan to close-in on a desired position if you know what forms a position plan.

The Hiring Position

Hiring position and Position Plan do not mean the same thing here. You need to understand that employer, not matter how big or small their company is; has something known as a Position Plan for the intended hiring position.

Your resume has to be best drafted to meet the Position Plan specified by the hiring manager. However, you will not know what is inside the Position Plan because what is available to you is only a hiring position on the job advertisement.

To demonstrate the correlation between the hiring position and a Position Plan, a common hiring position seen in job advertisement is illustrated below. The advertisement hopes to seek a successful Call Centre Engineer. We shall use this advertisement from 3KAgency for our case study purpose.

CALL CENTRE ENGINEER

RESPONSIBILITIES:

We seek an engineer who could provide excellent on-line customer technical support on PC desktop applications, operating systems and network operating systems, be able to undertake process improvement projects and management case escalation to third party service providers.

REQUIREMENT:
- Diploma in Engineering, Computer or Information Science, or other IT related discipline. Minimum 2 years of relevant working experience in technical or end-user-computing support environment. Either MCSE or CNE. Preferred but not essential.

- Proficient in PC software applications such as Microsoft Office Suite, Lotus Smart Suite and PC operating and network operating systems such as Microsoft Server 2000 and Windows XP.

- Flexibility in desk-bound and on-site assignments. Able to work on flexible hours.

- Excellent communications and internal personal, customer handling, trouble-shooting and analytical, and process skills

Interested? Kindly submit your resume with contact details, a recent photograph, your current and expected salary to our HR email: sabrina@3Kagency.com. Only short-listed candidate will be notified.

The Position Plan

The Position Plan of 3Kagency looks similar on the desk of the hiring manager but it has a more structured framework.

The Position Plan is made up of four key components, namely the MUST, WANT, FUNCTION and RESPONSIBILITY sections as illustrated in figure 3.1.

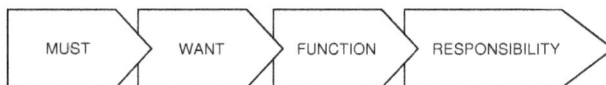

MUST > WANT > FUNCTION > RESPONSIBILITY >

Fig 3.1 Position Plan – 4 Essential Components

- The **MUST** describes the criteria that an ideal candidate should meet to qualify for the position.

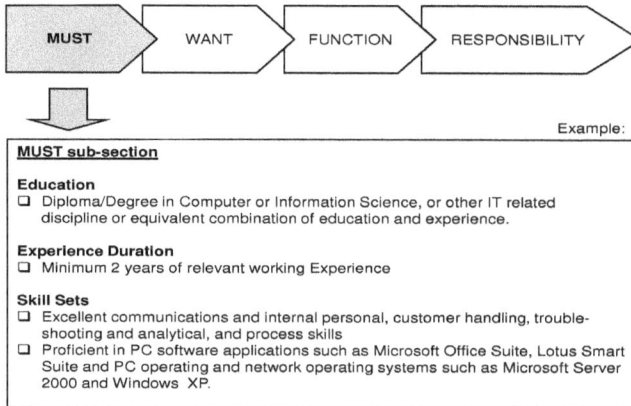

Fig 3.2 MUST sub-section.

- The **WANT** describes the "additional values" of a candidate. For example, ".... Fluent in Japanese speaking is an advantage...."

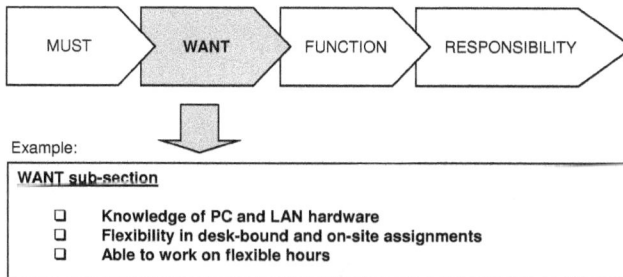

Fig 3.3. WANT sub-section

When two or more candidates fit all the **MUST** criteria, the WANT will help the hiring manager to narrow down on a particular candidate.

- **FUNCTION** describes your role in the position.

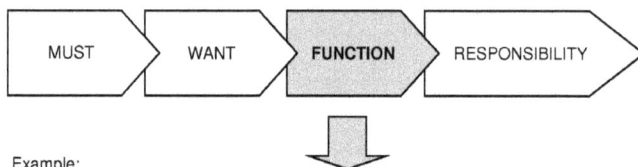

Fig 3.4 FUNCTION sub-section

- The **RESPONSIBILITY** describes the job ownership of the role specified.

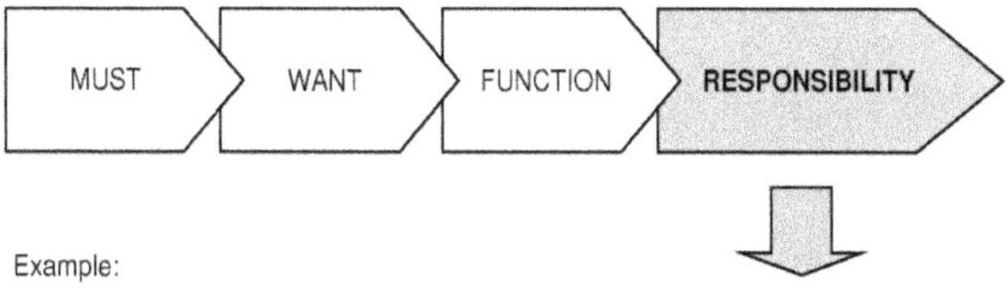

Example:

RESPONSIBILITY sub-section

❏ Provide excellent telephone support (i.e. usage assistance, fault isolation and problem solving) to customers' desktop computers, notebooks, peripherals and network products.
❏ Provide effective call management for problems not within scope of Call Center's expertise.
❏ Managed escalated cases to third party service providers and to be responsibility for successful closure and documentation.

Fig 3.5 RESPONSIBILITY sub-section

Exploiting The Position Plan

By positioning the 4 key components into a Resume Fit & Interview Fit matrix, it helps us to understand what hiring manager will be looking for in a resume.

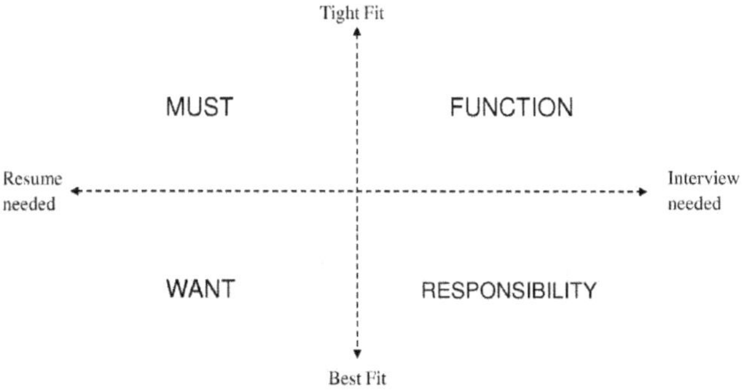

Fig 3.6 Resume Fit Vs Interview Fit Matrix

Must & Want

MUST is a stricter or tighter fit and WANT is a desirable fit.

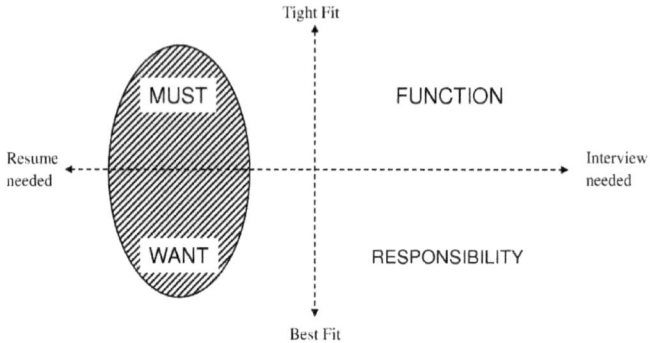

Fig. 3.7 MUST & WANT quadrants

Compare with FUNCTION and RESPONSIBILITY, MUST and WANT are the easier fit because the criteria are usually straight forward, tangible and measurable.

Examples:

- Bachelor degree in computer science (major in system analysis).
- 5 year experience in accounting, etc.

Function & Responsibility

The function of a job and therefore the responsibilities that you own are experience-based and without explaining yourself in an interview session, the hiring manager will not be able to qualify the match.

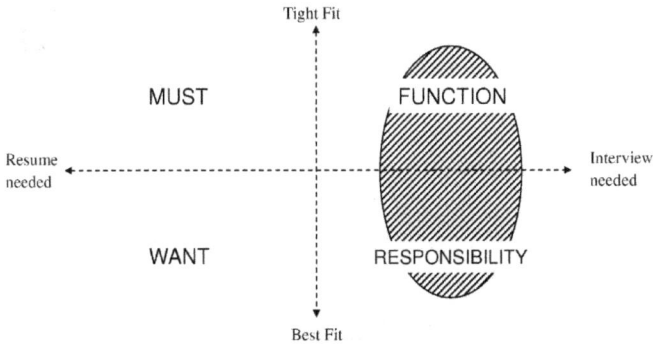

Fig. 3.8 FUNCTION & RESPONSIBILITY quadrants.

Must & Function

The matrix suggests that hiring manager will screen for tight fit criteria during their first-cut. The tight fit criteria, formed by MUST and FUNCTION' quadrants or the upper half of the matrix, has a greater "first-cut" weight-age over the lower half as shown in figure 3.9.

The more you work toward closing the gap between the MUST and FUNCTION quadrants, the better are your chances to be picked out during the first- cut resume screening.

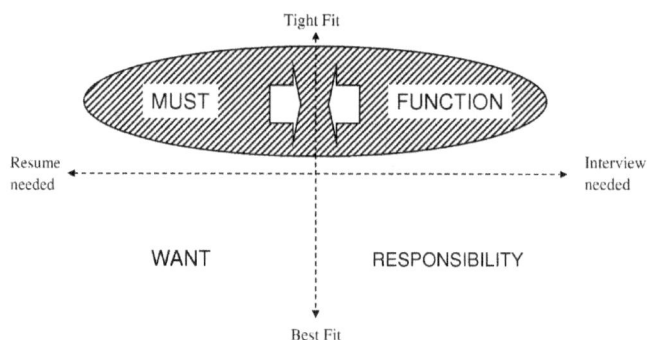

Tight Fit

MUST   FUNCTION

Resume needed ← - - - - - - - - - - - - - - - - - → Interview needed

WANT   RESPONSIBILITY

Best Fit

Fig. 3.9 MUST and FUNCTION quadrants

Ask yourself this question: If you know what the job functions and the MUST criteria expected by the prospective employer, would you have written your resume differently to best match the job expectation? Most would agree. So, fix this no. 1 problem in your resume if you have not done so.

Working Around Weak Fitting

If a job requires a bachelor degree but you hold a diploma with 5 years of experience, how are you going to let people knows that your 5 Year experience is above someone who has a degree without experience? Many weak fittings similar to this example have troubled a lot of candidates. It may also bother you because with 5 years experience, you would think that you are better than someone with a stronger academic background.

Interviews with a number of industries' hiring managers have suggested otherwise. Weak fitting does not discount a person from being hired. In a plain, simple case like the above example, the hiring manager will be keen to read your resume if you aim to voice out why you qualify for the position. Such justifications often emerge from the RESPONSIBILITY quadrant in the form of your accomplishments and achievements' which will proof your worth. But if you leave the justification until the interview session, then sadly, it may be too late. The up selling of you should begin from your resume. Together with predictable criteria listed in the MUST and FUNCTION quadrants, you should bring your resume towards getting the hiring manager's attention in the first-cut screening.

In the later part of the book, the Resume Sharpening techniques will switch you into the right gear of tweaking different components in the resume to overcome weak fitting.

Experience of Hiring Manager

The experience of the hiring manager has a lot to do with selection of candidates. For example, the MUST criteria is "must fit" in the eyes of many hiring managers. By running a candidate down the criteria, the process casts a safety net for managers to recruit the "right" candidate. Young hiring managers tends to rely on the criteria squarely to hire the right candidate.

Right candidate does not necessary mean the ideal candidate. Experienced managers will balance experience, academic, candidate' characteristics together with calculated risk to find the best fit. This explains the reason why 3KAgency published a looser criteria; accepting diploma or degree holder applicant. Unless the hirer has strict pre-requisite, for example, it is a must to hire degree holders for her clients. Nevertheless, you should attempt every opportunity to justify and close gap for the position you wanted.

Unhealthy Practices of Managers

Not all people are cut from Human Resource background. But when you are "Senior" enough in any position, hiring someone in a similar or identical capacity like yours can become part of your role. Candidate screening and successful interviews outcome are a whole lot of under-learned experience. Therefore, the experiences of "hiring" managers do vary.

Seasoned hiring managers who developed an "I think I know all about candidate screening" is a perspiring nightmare to candidates. These managers can stray off a professional interview, leaving unfruitful and very negative conclusion about a candidate.

(i) **Miscommunication**

A hiring manager looks for a good sales executive with an existing large customer base. As a candidate, you may wonder if "large" means many customers or few big customers.

And you described yourself as an outdoor promoter with "good sales track record". What you may really mean is an outdoor promoter with few sales but high sales dollar closure. For example, you sell Ball Retriever System for golf clubs.

But a hiring manager may wonder your "good" means many sales closed or few sales but high revenue turnovers? Interviewer and candidate should be specific what each other means.

You can avoid such miscommunication right from the start by writing clearly and concisely in the resume.

(ii)   **Unwritten Position Plan**

When a hiring manager has a preferred type of candidates in his mindset, an "Unwritten Position Plan" may exist to form part of his recruiting behavior and practice. Unwritten Position Plan is the dirty-product of self-perception outside the written position plan.

For example, one candidate came in for an interview with a bandaged broken leg. The hiring manager rejected the candidate politely. Since the candidate met all the hiring criteria, I checked for the reason why. The explanation was a bandaged candidate inferred "carelessness" and will be prone to disrupt work very often.

Listen to this next story. A female candidate turned up for an interview with her boyfriend. While the interview was conducted between the hiring manager and the candidate, the boyfriend waited outside the interview room. Do you know that this candidate was "rejected" right from the start? I asked the hiring manager why he rejected the candidate. The answer was accompanied candidate is not independent.

Hiring Manager Looks for Solid Stuff

Hiring managers looks for skills that match the job description. But professional hiring managers look for evidences in the resume that suggest a candidate will bring essential skills transfer from previous career into the current job.

(i) **Transferable Skills**

Transferable Skills of a candidate are skills that do not deteriorate over time. Skills like customer services, business skill, auditing skill, writing skill, computing programming skill etc. all fall into this category. The more you practice them in your career, the better you are. And you need to bring out these skills in your resume.

Take computer programming as an example. Is programming skill transferable? For any new computer language, you cannot run away from learning it. But the programming fundamentals remain the same. It is common for candidates to be astounded when the hiring manager asked if they are familiar with an alien programming language. I knew the candidates' minds went blank whenever they were asked; they gave silly trembling answers. For example,

"It is something like J2EE? I learned it only during my university but never get to use it in my work."

Does hiring manager want to hear the programming language you don't know? The hiring manager really wants to know how convincing you are to transfer you existing skill to the new programming language.

You can try answering the question like this: "Programming is easy. Your language sound familiar to me. Let me to pick up the language in a week or two. The rest is more like picking up as I learn on the job."

Since we are on the subject of programming, these Gurus ended up chocking me with how many projects they did, what these projects are all about and how long they took to finish them. Their stories went on and on; some filling over 20 pages of their resumes. Hiring managers are poor story listener but good fact sniffer; Whenever you find that a hiring manager try to disrupt your story-telling by asking a question or two, trust me, they want you to stop.

Having many projects simply means that you have a wealth of experience. Try connecting the projects and make them look transferrable. For example,

"My knowledge of Accounting is acquired from developing software modules to capture tax policy changes due to FTA."

This simply statement implies that knowledge of accounting is transferable)

(ii) Accomplishment Record

This book makes a clear distinction between accomplishment and achievement. Accomplishment is the fulfillment of the roles and the responsibilities which an employer expected from an employee. Quite bluntly, you get paid only if you meet this roles and responsibilities.

When you understand accomplishment as your roles and responsibilities, it easier for you to see how your previous experience can match a new advertised position. If you describe your previous accomplishments closely to the job advertised, the hiring manager will be keen to interview you to further ascertain your skill can be best transferred to his organization or at least be repeated.

During the interview, all you have to do is to prepare facts, cases and examples that support your previous job roles and responsibilities. This will sufficiently create a mental picture with the hiring manager whether you can "repeat" the accomplishments in the new position.

A 100 percent accomplishment fit is not something to be excited about. This only means that if you are hired, you are essentially doing the same job all over again. And someday when you get tired, you will leave the job once more. Re-hiring and training new staff is very painfully and costly for many companies. What else does the hiring manager look for inside your resume?

(iii) Repeatable Achievement

Although the technique for writing accomplishment and achievement may be similar, "achievement" actually records the uniqueness above the usual accomplishments. For example, if you can reduce the usual account closing period from 7 days to 3 days through use of computers, this is clearly an achievement.

Similar to repeatable skills, hiring manager has the tendency to drill into your achievements if you are a repeating achiever in the new job. This requires a different form of writing in the resume. This technique of qualitative writing is discussed in the chapter "Cover Letter".

You may have mistaken that achievements can only be derived from innovations or greater productivity improvements. I will share with you that this is not so in Chapter 9 Thinking and Training Our Minds to "See" Achievement.

In this book, I urge readers to focus a lot on Achievements throughout the course of your career.

RESUME SHARPENING

CHAPTER 4
THE THREE WRITE RULES

Rule #1: Write To Prepare for Interview

Writing resume and preparing for interview are interconnected activities. There is no better way to walk through your career flashback than to write them down. When you carefully walk through your thoughts, you bring the bits and pieces together, telling yourself specifically where are your strength and what your past achievements are and what your accomplishments are. And jointly with your next job in mind, you build a resume around your goals and career plan. You deliberately forced yourself to think-through and recite through what you will say during an interview.

A resume is a blue print on how you will answer questions about yourself during a job interview. This is important because hiring manager will attempt to clarify anything that is unclear in your resume and you need to prepare answers even before the interview.

When I coached a class of working executives sometime back in year 2002, one executive raised this question: How are we going to anticipate what questions a hiring manager will ask during a job interview? I told him that a hiring manager can ask any question and put it to you in any form; you will tilt the boat and capsize if you cannot answer a question pertaining to yourself. This is especially so if that question comes directly from your resume. That is an absolute embarrassment!

For example, you claimed yourself to be a creative person in your resume but when you attempt to answer the following questions, do you stumble?

Why do you think you are a creative person? Gave an example of something you have done before that you think it is creative?
If the answers do not come to you instantly, the game may be over! Let extend it to another 5 more minutes. You think about it and try answering the same question again. Have your got some answers but it is still fuzzy in your mind? The interview can be over!

There is a big difference between "You know" and "You think you know". The latter is often the adopted mentality in a lot of us! Conveniently, we assumed that things we did previously must automatically stay in our mind forever. In actual fact, you lose those memories faster than you can recall them.

You need to recall and upkeep your memories by dry-run the thinking process and the best way to do it is to physically run it down on your resume.

The more you elaborate what is written in a resume and relate them to your own experiences, the better you are in crystallizing your said experiences. This memory-mining process is better reinforced and recited in writing; better than capturing floating memories in your head. You may end up forgetting or unable to recall them in the middle of a job interview.

Rule #2: Write First-Cut Resume

"First Cut" is an essential screening process to filter out the right candidate from the piles of resumes. This repetitive process can be tedious when applicants get voluminous. Imagine you are the human resource manager and you have to go through a handful of resumes. No sooner will all resumes look alike. Professional hirer will browse through resumes, pick and "digest" only the selected resumes i.e. the hirer did a "first cut" filtering effort. On the "second cut", he decides who he wants to conduct a face to face interview. If your resume slips through during the first cut, chances are that your resume will never be re-visited. Therefore, a well formulated first-cut resume can increase the chances of being caught by the hiring manager.

Your resume has to be drafted in a way to attract the hiring manager when he does his first cut. To maximize your chance to be caught during the "first cut" process, a resume will need these key attributes:

(a)   "Cosmetics" Look and Feel

Look and Feel relates to your overall resume turnout. A clear and concise resume structure allows easy access to information.

(b)   Avoid:

- Lengthy resume
- Cluttered content
- Long paragraphs
- Lack of indentation, bold print
- Lack of universal order style, for example, from oldest hiring to the most recent.

(c)   Generous But Careful Use of "Eye-Catching" Words.

A resume tell people about you. With zero face to face contact with your prospective employer, your resume needs to work like a "marketing brochure" to attract attention and "shout the loudest" that you are the best for the job. Knowing the hiring manager skims through resume during their "first-cut", catchy words in your resume increase reading pleasure and encourage mind and eye focus on targeted facts. Figure 4.1 illustrates an example.

Plain Version	Re-written Version
"I was a captain in the school's basket ball team that won a number of awards."	"I was a captain in the school's basket ball team, leading several inter-states games; winning one gold and two silvers in the final two years."

Fig 4.1 Eye-Catching Words

Are you able to spot the "eye-catching" words? **Lead**, **Winning**, **Gold**, **Silvers** and **Final two Years**?

Therefore, as a market brochure about you, a resume should be proliferated with "eye-catching" words.

(i)   A True Story

Hasmin (not his real name) and I have fulfilled a two and half years of national service in my country. Hasmin was an admin clerk and I was a technical specialist.

1st May 1992 was Hasmin's last day to complete his service. On that evening, we were on a public bus back home. Hasmin sat beside me and he spoke to me about his future.

Hasmin was unhappy about his logistics role as a clerk. And now he had completed his national "liability", he looked forward to work in the commercial industry that maximizes his potential and talent. He felt that national service is an absolutely waste of time. And now that he is going to find a job, he will need a resume. But he cannot help himself to write a good resume based on his wasted years in national service.

Although what I did was different from Hasmin to serve the nation, there was something badly wrong about him not holding pride in what he did for his country. And I said these to him:

"Hasmin, it is not about yourself in your national service. It is about us. You need to understand or at least appreciate how your unit co-existed with other units to form one national defense. The service and the work you discharged, allowed you to feel and felt this national defense by contributing a small part during your tour of duty"

Hasmin giggled immediately after what I said. But he thought for a moment and confessed: "I felt patriotic after you said those words". We spoke very little for the rest of our journey.

A few months later, Hasmin sent me a thank-you note with this little cut-out from his resume:

"I have fully discharged a dedicated clerical role during my two and half years of nation service. Every day was a well learned day about national defense."

Do you see the "eye-catching" words popping out in front of you: **DEDICATED** and **WELL LEARNED?**

(ii) **"Eye-Catching" Word, Not Again?**

Many job seekers often mistook "eye-catching" words for bombastic catch phases, teasing words, bull shitting, marketing gimmick and cheap low-form of "copywriting" technique. I called this the "ballooning" effect. This is like telling people how big your balloon is without telling them what gas is filled inside. Take a look at this example in figure 4.2 and see you can spot ballooning effect:

The candidate is an experience chef for many renowned restaurants / hotels in Asia Pacific.

F&B Outlet Setting Experience:

- Jakarta, <restaurant name #1>, Full set up of a brand new established seated capacity of 200 pax Fine Chinese Dining Hall & Kitchen

---

- Singapore, <restaurant name #2>, Full set up of a seating capacity 330 pax Fine Dinning Hall & Kitchen
- Singapore, <restaurant name #3>, mini kitchen set up
- Manila, <Restaurant name #4>, Full Kitchen set up for the Grand Ballroom
- Singapore, <restaurant name #5>, Full set up of a seating capacity 220 pax Fine Chinese Dining Hall & Kitchen

Fig. 4.2 Extract from an experienced F&B candidate's resume

In the paragraph above, the candidate aims to tell the prospective employer his past experience in restaurant set up and he went down the list using eye-catching words like "full set up", "new established" and size of seating capacity etc. to demonstrate his depth of knowledge. They look good for one moment. But what is a "full set up"? "Full set up" is used almost in each bullet points and yet not quite explaining itself. Does "full setup" mean equipment setup, manpower hiring, process definition, menu design or what? All these words are used without an explanation. This is a "ballooning" effect example.

"Eye-Catching" word buys attention. Although we can use it generously but what you claimed must be supported by facts and evidences to add creditability. Otherwise, you are right that are just bombastic catch phases.

Rule #3: Writing About Yourself

Good written resume does not necessary mean that you have good writing skill. Students that went through my resume-writing classes had a different conclusion: it is all about knowing what to write. You are writing about yourself and nothing else. All you have to do is to pick up simple and concise words to say about yourself, know what to say and when to say it.

Good writing skill alone cannot make your resume stand out. If the job requires the power of your language and strong writing skill, it makes sense for hiring manager to scan for well written sentences in the language. But when you have a well written resume, it is language independent because it will carry the facts that describe you and your career in a fashion that bring attention to hiring manager. In the simplest form, you could write about yourself in bulleted points.

CHAPTER 5
SIMPLE BUT GOOD RESUME LAYOUT

If you have been doing research on books that tells you how to write the perfect resume layout, you should realize that no matter how you change the format, the key components in a resume remain the same relatively. For instance, no one will tell you to leave out the academic history section in a resume.

Unlike most conventional resume layout that contains exhaustive list of areas believe to cover every aspect of you, Figure 5.1 shows a sample resume layout containing the crucial components needed in a resume.

Boxed into 3 major sections, namely the Header, the Body and the Footer, each section is discussed in a light to alert you on the Why and the What of each components, important enough to catch the attention of your reader.

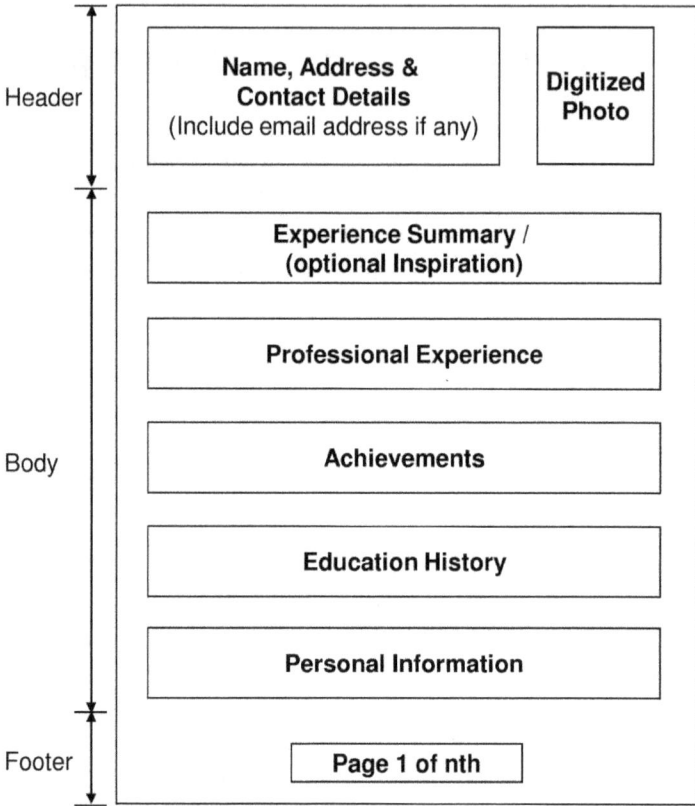

Fig 6.1 Sample of Resume Layout

Header Section

The Header section carries your name, address contact details and a photograph of you. The Header is unique in many ways:

- Do **NOT** print a title at your header section. Everyone knows this is a resume. You need not say "Curriculum Vitae". Often, candidate feels that these titles are important and they print them in large-size font. Ask yourself: How does the big title add value to your resume?

- Use the header's space to advertise yourself. How? Remember, the top left and right most column of your local newspaper is occupy by miniature, expensive advertisement? Fill this column with your name (use standard naming order, for example, first name, last name), mailing address, all possible contact numbers and your e-mail address, if any.

- Place your digitized photo on the header's space. That will save you cost instead of sending real photo to prospective employers.

  Be "appropriate" in your photo turnout. For example, for an executive position, a clean and formal outlook is highly desirable.

Also, make sure that your digitized photo is reasonable sized (passport size preferred) with good resolution. Gray scale image caters a wide audience because most desktop / laser printers are able to handle black color printing.

- Advertise the same header content on every page of your resume. Why? If one or more of the resume' pages drop out, the hiring manager may not locate all the pages but he/she is still able to locate you.

Body Section

The Body section contains 5 sub-sections, each for a strong purpose appearing in a strategic order. The order which your "story" unfold is really your call. But there is some precedence you may want to take note.

- Experience Summary (and Inspiration) often takes the top storyline. With an opening that talks about experience, we did not say it needs to be working experience. The way to capitalize on overhead banner like Experience Summary is to shout it loud to your intended reader about what you are really good in. If it has to be working experience, whatever your shout needs to be relevant to the job. A poor example is "I am good at something....". You are supposed to shout and give the proof at the same time. A good example will be "I am good at something because I have 5 years of experience in ....".

Some candidates include another paragraph to describe their inspiration, particularly, Career Inspiration. If you think Experience Summary is factual, then Inspiration is the reverse. Inspiration statements are often made to work around weak connections; making them sound positive. For example, I inspired to be "project manager in 5 year time ..." and you jolly know well that you are only half way there. Inspiration statements can be used dangerously without supportive elements to back it up. Using the same example, you could rewrite like this: "I inspired to be a project manager in 5 years times because I voluntarily take up leadership role whenever it come to working in a team."

- Some candidates arrange Education History above Professional Experience. Normally, when your strength lies in one of the sub-section but not the other, you will position the stronger sub-section at the top to maximize visibility. For example, a fresh graduate will rank Education History above Profession Experience sub-section. In contrast, a less-academic individual will rank his Professional Experience above Education History sub-section.

- Some candidates may combine "Personal Information" with the Header. In country like India where the immediate family, extended families and relatives have prestige statuses in the society, the candidate will first associate with the affluences before addressing himself. Unfortunately, this is not quite the usual practices in contemporary Human Resources.

Working "Experience Summary"

This top paragraph in a resume allows you to give an overview of your working experience. Because this paragraph provides a summary of your career, it becomes a convenient location for a hiring manager to grasp your working experience in the first-cut screening. The visual format you chose for this paragraph become very important. Compare the two approaches below and pick the one that catches your attention if you only have 5 to 10 seconds?

"My past career span over 6 years after my university degree in summer 2002 and I begin to work in small firm <**Company #1>** picking up audit practices and field training. This was following by a year and half working as Financial Analyst with one of the big five <**Company #2>**."

Period	Job Title	Employer	Roles
2009 - 2008	Financial Analyst	Company #2	
2008 – 2002	Auditor	Company #1	

The tablet approach serves well at the beginning of a resume aiding the hiring manager in assessing your experience based on the number of working years. This is the quantitative visual. The same location can also be replaced by a narrative paragraph whenever the job applied looks at the power of language as a passing criterion. This is the qualitative visual. When you lack of working experiences or your total working experiences does not portrait you well for hiring, the qualitative visual (narrative version) helps to bring out your other non-quantitative strength. But when you got nothing quantitative or qualitative to explain your good-self, go jump to chapter 7 for tactical techniques to write Working Experience Summary.

Cohabiting together at this upper location, you may furnish a short paragraph on career inspiration especially when you are switching into a different and unfamiliar career. Career inspiration elicits your passion and interest for the job or the industry that the job was related. Therefore, this paragraph will favor you when working experience is weak or irreverent. Hiring managers are well aware of the cost to fire and re-hire. Your career inspiration gives the hiring manager another reason why he chooses you instead of a competing candidate who does not express mid- to-long term career interest.

Professional Experience

Begin with the most current experience, you describes the roles and responsibilities in each of your milestones in chronological order. Remembered not too long ago, we discussed Accomplishment and Achievement was meant to be different altogether. If you really need to speak how well you did in certain role that went beyond responsibilities, write only Accomplishment statements here. This intentionally leaves all your achievements in a separate section called Achievements. Some candidates prefer to write accomplishments and achievements within a profession experience to indicate the relevance to the profession. This is not wrong. However, there is always a danger when you embed or "camouflage" accomplishments and achievements in between roles and responsibilities statements. This will make your achievements less visible during the first-cut screening.

Education History

Your academics are compacted inside this section. I used the word "compacted" because I felt that you only need to tell the hiring manager your highest academic attained and the industry-training you received that are most relevant to the job applied. For example, there is no factual objective when candidate tell me where and when you begin your primary school. Your highest academic achievement only demonstrates you have gone through several years of academic thinking in a particular field or level of study. Similarly, your industry training or certification means you have gone deep into specialized training in well-defined environment. Hiring managers take the academic data as pre-requisite into qualifying for first-cut matches.

Some candidates are too shy to include their poor academic scores in their resume. If poor academic result will do you more harm, I suggest that you leave your academic result out of the resume. In situation that favor you, only then academic scores will be provided.

To write Education History is another form of writing achievements. In this context, it is about Academic achievements. However, academic alone will not stand you out from the crowd. It is therefore imperative to elaborate more in the Professional Experience section and the Achievement section.

You can flip the position of Education History sub-section to come before Professional Experience especially you are a fresh graduate. This will bring your academic records up to the front to have precedence over the weaker Professional Experience.

If you have been working for many years, work experiences become the selling points. However, some people have a long list of working experiences that most hiring managers would treat is like frequent job hopping. Chapter 7 and 8 will deal with such strapping issues and turn it in favor of you. Back to the positioning, it is all about making a sensible choice how you position your education and experience so that it reflects you in the better light.

Achievements

Achievement section is all about describing your "winnings" in professional endeavors. Though easy to speak, but not many people can differentiate accomplishment from achievement. Chapter 9 will share the differences and why you need to think achievement most of the time.

On the notion that you are able to repeat and champion in what you achieve before, cleverly-crafted Achievement section will map your "winnings" not by career progression but the targeted purpose to win a job. Chapter 9 also shows how grouping technique is used for this purpose.

Writing achievement statement is both science and art. Chapter 10 shows you how achievement statements are constructed using a simple syntax that covers breadth, depth or both using factual information.

Personal Information

This sub-section will carry your personal particulars. You might realize that "Personal Information", a sub-section that appears top in many resumes, now become the last. Your resume is a self-marketing brochure. The lucrative "products and services" are your experience and achievements. Therefore, the "lucrative merchandises" come first. This is again a personal preference.

Footer Section

Be sure the pages are labeled correctly i.e. the page number and the total number of pages.

Resume Length

Most hiring manager "scans" resume. During a "first cut", would you scan a 2 page or a 5 page resume? The answer is obvious. A shorter resume does have an edge over the long, "windy" one.

A recommended resume length is 1 to 2 (A4) pages. But if you absolutely need to write, keep it no more than 4 pages.

Consider trimming down the resume length, here are some helpful tips:

- You may have discovered a lot about yourself after applying the resume writing technique. But you may be cluttering the resume with information not relevant to the targeted job.

- You may have a long career history i.e. various key appointments or many jobs. Or is it plenty of job switches?

- You may have so much roles and responsibilities that without writing them down, you are afraid that someone will miss it.

- You will discover in later part of the book, achievements are imperative part of the resume more than roles, responsibilities and accomplishments.

- You may have many achievements in your career. Would you consider writing just the top 3 achievements from each job?

To wrap up this chapter, you will need to get your resume ready. For those without a resume, you may begin with a draft script about yourself and break them down by sections and sub-sections following the sample resume layout. Do not border about how well you write at this point. The priority task is to get the bits and pieces in the right position within a resume.

CHAPTER 6
PREPARING FOR RESUME
SHARPENING

In the next few chapters, I will demonstrate tactical writing techniques to sharpen dull resume into up-selling personal brochure. Explicitly, they are creative writing techniques for non-friction and damn serious purpose. I will introduce a collective of techniques that can vastly apply to any of the sections and sub-sections in the resume. For demonstration and teaching purpose, I have to limit to a few important sections to make sure your resume can take-off immediately once it is completed.

In each of these sections, the writing technique is meant to drive out under-selling about you. In early part of the book, I emphasized that for every statement you write in the resume, you will need to support it with a compelling story — fact-base approach. Therefore, seeking fact-base support naturally forms a self checking mechanism that prevents you from over-selling yourself as well. Incidentally, if the statement you write sound "bombastic" or "over-selling" to the reader, it only means you get too carried away when you write your resume. Most of the time, you will not realize it. Therefore, it is better than once you get the resume written, find someone to read it. Don't ask your parent to read it. They will think it all alright because they are too proud of their children. Ask a genuine friend who will humbly point out the "over-selling" and ask you to explain the facts underlying the over-sold.

To benefit a lot more from these techniques, I urge you to put a copy of your resume side by side and work along with the techniques as they unfold. As we move along, you will gauge for yourself if the resume makes improvement progressively. In the classes I had conducted, the techniques had allowed the students to discover a lot more about them and went a long way in helping them to craft resumes in most compelling way.

As you move from one technique to another, you will notice that these techniques are purely creative writing techniques. In other words, you do not have to restraint one technique to just one part of the resume. Past students have learned to apply techniques across different sections of the resume based on context, needs and flow.

I said before that as you think through how you resume is written i.e. you are physically "walking-through" the connecting events, accomplishment and achievements which map up your great, grand story. You are mentally rehearsing what possibly could be dug up about you during an interview.

Walking-through creates a deeper impression in your mind. So, the next time when you are called up for interview, do you think you can recall them better? Obviously, No! Before each interview, you need to walk-through the resume again as a refresher so that "recalling" takes lesser effort every time and interconnecting all past and the current events are very clear in your mind. Your diligent preparation will pay off when your win the job.

CHAPTER 7
STRATEGIES FOR WRITING
"WORKING EXPERIENCE
SUMMARY"

The Working Experience Summary is an overview of your career most relevant to the job applied. A good tailored Working Experience Summary allows the hiring manager to connect your skill and talent to the hiring position at the very early stage of resume screening.

But can you do away with a Working Experience Summary? Without a summary section, you actually give the hiring manager a harder time. How? The hiring manager will look into your career history to look for time based information and aggregate them to become meaningful data that he can make sound judgment if you fit the job. This is very logical because most hiring managers will conveniently use the number of years a candidate spent in a particular profession (or specialized field) to rank your seniority and experience. Without a Working

Experience Summary, the hiring manager will need to pick up bits and pieces from your employment records to do his job properly. If this is the case, you might as well pamper him with a summary that he can obtain time-based information. It is important, therefore, that this summary should be a concise capsule form, sometimes under 5 lines of text.

In addition, the summary describes only your relevant skill or talent while keeping the less desirable ones out of the picture. We are by no means to hide, lie or deceive except lying low until being question.

There are a few strategies to build Working Experience Summary:

Skill-Based, Time-Based Approach

This is a very easy approach for hiring manager who is looking for factual based information to consider you as a prospective candidate. You will list your skills and within each skill, you label your years of experiences. Fig 7.1 is an example.

Programming	Visual Basic	3 years+
	C++, Java	1.5 years
	SQL	1.5 years
	.NET, VB	Self Study > 1 year
Hardware	Unix-based Server (Admin, SQL)	1.5 years
	Personal Computer Repair	3 years

Fig. 7.1 Skill based, Time based Approach

Industry-Focus Approach

This approach requires all your employment records in the same industry to be consolidated and quantified by the total number of years spent in that industry.

In figure 7.2, a project manager in Company A took up a sales & marketing role in The Sales Division of Company B. Both Company A & B business are in Information Technology.

Industry (IND)	Company A	Company B
Information Technology	Project Manager	Sales Manager

Fig 7.2 Industry-Focus Approach Working Summary

Hybrid Approach

Hybrid matrix is a tool to represent your experiences using functional roles across industries. A complex pictorial form is shown in figure 7.3.

Industry (IND)	Time Based, Skill Based (TS)		
	TS #1	TS#2	TS#3
IND#1	Hybrid #1	Hybrid #3	Hybrid #4
IND#2			Hybrid #5
IND#3	Hybrid #2		

Fig 7.3 Hybrid Approach

By combining time-based, skill based and industry-focus approaches, you can co-relate or pull two or more scattered experiences in different industries together to elicit a progressive acquisition of skills.

In the example shown in Fig. 7.4 below, Joanne - a copier's Sales Engineer was a research assistant in the biotech industry.

Industry (IND)	Time Based, Skill Based (TS)	
	TS#1 1 year Sales	TS#2 2 Years Research
IND #1 Copier Company	Sales Engineer	N.A.
IND#2 Biotech Company	N.A.	Research Assistant

Fig.7.4 Hybrid Approach (Before Co-relation)

Think of the hybrid approach as such: when the Time-based, Skilled-Based roles cut across the industries, a new functional role may be surfaced.

In Fig. 7.5, we deliberately correlated the past experience across industries to review a accumulated skill sets.

Industry	Time Based, Skill Based (TS)	
(IND)	TS#1 1 year Sales	TS#2 2 Years Research
IND #1 Copier Company	**Hybrid #1** **Ask yourself this:** **(a) Do co-related skills make sense and relevant to the job you applied?**	
IND#2 Biotech Company	**(b) Are they just complimentary skills i.e. difficult to co-relate in anyway?**	

Fig. 7.5 Hybrid Approach (After Co-relation)

Each time you attempt a co-relation between 2 or more past experiences, you have to ask yourself if the correlated skill sets make sense and relevant to the type of jobs you applied.

Creative Use of Hybrid Approach

Supposing a Ms Mary Boustead (not her real name) has been working for the past 15 years and the recent last 3 jobs were described briefly below.

2000 – 2002 (3 Years)	Customer Account Manager with IT Company A
1997 – 2000 (3 Years)	Teacher - Teaches Art and Social Science in High School
1995 – 1997 (3 Years)	Sales & Marketing Engineer with IT Company B

Fig. 7.6 Ms Mary Boustead's Recent Working History.

Ms Mary Boustead held a total of 6 years in the Information technology (IT) industry verse a 3 year teaching job. Ms Mary Boustead's working experience can be manipulated using the hybrid approach to suit different job application.

(a)   Information Technology

Mary utilizes her 6 years of IT experience fully to support her job application. Fig. 7.7 illustrates the functional mapping across 2 companies which Mary had worked. The black shaded area means a higher percentage co-relation between the experiences.

Industry	Time Based, Skill Based		
	3 Years , Cust. Acc. Management	3 Years, Sales & Marketing	3 Years, Teaching
IT Company A	**Information technology Skill**		
IT Company B			
Education			
Skill Relevance	<<Most>>	<<Most>>	

Fig 7.7 Hybrid Approach – Information Tech.

Then, she wrote her Working Experience Summary as such: "With 6 years of experience in Information Technology, I have acquired a unique know-how of the industry and I hope to bring in sales and manage customers for the employer I work for."

(b)   Management Executive

In applying for a Management Executive position, all 9 years of experience across 3 companies were pulled together. And she wrote: "With 9 years of experience, I am progressively instilled with a wide range of useful business skills: from a humble sales position, teaching cum training to service large customers' accounts."

Industry	Time Based, Skill Based		
	3 Years, Cust. Acc. Management	3 Years, Sales & Marketing	3 Years, Teaching
IT Company A	**Manage-ment Skill**	**Complimentary Skills**	
IT Company B			
Education			
Skill Relevance	<<Most	Moderate	Least>>

Fig 7.8 Hybrid Approach – Management Executive

Fig. 7.8 illustrates this concept. Note that the skill co-relates stronger on the left and grey out on the right.

(c) Training and Teaching Skill

Mary's working experience can be stretched further to place Mary in the light of a teaching profession as shown in fig. 7.9.

Industry	Time Based, Skill Based		
	3 Years, Cust. Acc. Management	3 Years, Sales & Marketing	3 Years, Teaching
IT Company A			
IT Company B			
Education	Complimentary Skills		Teaching Skill
Skill Relevance	<<Moderate	Moderate	Most >>

Fig. 7.9 Hybrid Approach - Teaching

She wrote: "I am a teacher by profession for 3 years but I can undertake more than teaching because I was enriched by another 6 years of hands-on experience, holding different positions in the industry that can possibly add on to the education value-chain."

The more you practices on writing Working Experience Summary, you will automatically incline to one of the approaches that best suit you.

To conclude this section, begin by writing your Working Experience Summary using the techniques discussed. Most people begin with Time based, Skill based or the Industry-focus approach. Not everyone experiences can be easily translated into hybrid approach. You may want to seek further help from the author if your experiences can be co-related.

CHAPTER 8
STRATEGIES FOR WRITING
"PROFESSIONAL EXPERIENCE"

Most resumes, if not all, will have a *Professional Experiences* section. However, they are usually not written in a way for a hiring manager to sniff out the right candidate quickly. I have taken close examination at the *Professional Experience* section of many resumes and would like to point out these common mistakes:

- Working experience written in reversed chronological order i.e. starting from the earliest employment at the top and only allowing the most recent experiences to surface last.

- A direct copy of the roles and responsibilities from the employee's appointment letter. The content is often too generic and tells little about their personal contribution on the job.

- It is common for a person to have a similar roles and responsibilities from one employment to another. However, in describing your roles and responsibilities, they cut and past the identical paragraph for each and every similar employment; making the entire Professional Experience section looks uninteresting.

- There is a serious lack of achievement statements in most of the resumes I came across.

- Roles, responsibilities, accomplishment and achievements statements are condensed into a single long paragraph. The candidate's selling points become very hard to be spotted during first-cut screening.

A separately-written paragraph for Roles and Responsibilities, Accomplishment and then Achievement will be a better approach to help you structure what you want to say in each career. Incidentally, this method serves very well for hiring manager to pick up who his candidates are during the first cut screening.

Professional Experience is commonly accepted as a narration around the roles and responsibilities assigned during an employment. In the context of this book, *Professional Experience* refers to the results derived from a career's roles and responsibilities explicitly. The result is known as *Accomplishment.* In this chapter, we will discuss *Accomplishment* only, We shall leave *Achievement* discussion until the next chapter.

"Roles and Responsibilities" is not equal to Accomplishment

Accomplishment is the result derived from roles and responsibilities (R&R). Because of this differentiation, Accomplishment will automatically fire-up the resume by telling the hiring manager to see the results first.

To illustrate the power of writing Accomplishment, figure 8.3 shows an example on how a simple role and responsibility is turned into a powerful accomplishment statement.

Style of Writing	Written Examples	Remarks
Roles and Responsibilities Focus	"Generate month-end report."	Plain definition of role & responsibility. Ownership, timeliness and repeatability information are missing.
Accomplishment Focus	"I completed month-end reporting on time every month."	The result of roles and responsibilities carried out. (1) Ownership = "I" (2) Repeatability = "every month" (3) Timeliness = "On-time"

Fig. 8.1 Roles & Responsibilities Vs Accomplishment

The Accomplishment-focus style is a vast improvement over the classic R&R. The reason is obvious; the hiring manager looks for repeatable and transferable skills in the most logical way as he reads a resume.

Functional Writing Style

Professional Experience paragraph can sometime be so clutter by mixing roles, responsibilities and accomplishments altogether. Clarity can be improved by grouping the relevant experiences within functional headings that are closely associated with popular industry terms.

To illustrate an example, Teena (not her real name) has a dream job – a Fine-Dining Restaurant Manager. Before she applies for the position, Teena has lots of related experiences as shown in figure 8.2 – a partial extraction from her resume without any touch up.

Classic Writing Style
Working Experience
• At the age of 28, she started her first restaurant in central part of \<country name\> as the capital of $XXX('000) in

1995.

- She started from zero and learned to perform every duties of operation whenever there was a shortage of manpower.

- She set up her second, third & fourth restaurants in eastern, western part of <country #3> in the following 3 year time.

- She studied every possible factors that may help to increase the volume of business. All these tough jobs & duties were continuously carried out days by days before she saw profit awarded.

- She pushed the revenue to exceed $ YYY('000) in the first seventeen months.

- Her husband who was a 20 over year experienced executive chef in Fine Chinese dining, practically trained the kitchen staffs proper Chinese food processing skill.

  - Various working experiences as follow:

    - Dealing operation in commodities firm (company #1)
    - Stock & Inventory control

> (company#2)
> - Cost Accounting (company #3)

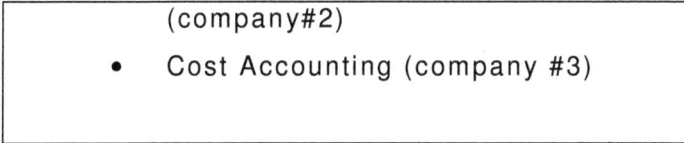

Fig 8.2 Classic Writing Style – Written in an active voice.

The writing style that Teena adopted is narrative story telling. If the entire text in figure 8.2 is collapse, you will enjoy reading a story essay. There is nothing wrong with the story-writing style.

In fact, even in bullet point form, it is perfectly alright. Whenever a candidate has difficulties to write or if he is weak in phrasing compelling paragraphs, the bullet point form is the most useful.

However, there is a better way to deal with cluttering using bullet point by focusing on function skills.

Figure 8.3 shows a polished version where the cluttering is broken down into clear, functional roles.

Functional Writing Style

Professional Experience 1995-1998

Restaurant Entrepreneurship

Despite a humbly background with no formal academic training, Teena owned a total of 4 Chinese Restaurant between 1995 and 1998. Supported by her husband, a Master Chef of Chinese Cuisine, Teena literally turned her initial investment of $XXX('000) into close to $YYY ('000) sales revenue in two and a half years of restaurant operation.

Operation Management

In restaurant operation, Teena is a highly effective manager. From supply ordering, manpower utilization, food utilization, inventory management and financial accounting, Teena's restaurant management style is prudent, revenue cum profit generating and winning customer satisfaction.

Fig 8.3 Functional Writing Style

Teena's experience falls under 2 popular key roles: Restaurant Entrepreneurship and Operation Management. Both titles represent key attributes of a restaurant-dinning manager and will be picked up quickly by hiring manager during the first-cut screening. The content is centered on the 2 functional titles to support their purposes and further provide the facts below them. Within each functional paragraph, Teena provides the evidence to support the functional headings.

Titanium CV

CHAPTER 9

THINKING AND TRAINING OUR MINDS TO "SEE" ACHIEVEMENT

Accomplishment and Achievement are commonly used interchangeable and often treated as they mean the same thing. In this book, I have deliberately defined Achievement very different from Accomplishment. By doing so, it becomes much easier to see if you are writing about your roles, responsibilities, accomplishment or are you really writing about your achievements.

The illustration below demonstrates a sharp contrast between Accomplishment and Achievement.

Accomplishment	*Achievement*
A person who completes month-end reporting on time every month.	A person discovered a way to do month end reporting on half the usual time.

Fig 9.1 Accomplishment Vs Achievement

"Accomplishment" Definition

Job accomplishment is the result of your roles and responsibilities. The job responsibility is therefore to generate month-end report on time.

"Achievement" Definition

Job achievement is a way to describe a job accomplishment done in some unique fashion. In this example, "half the usual time" gives a quantitative distinction from a plain job accomplishment.

I may give the first impression that Achievement statement is writing about innovation found on the job. That will be very difficult for everyone especially if you are not inventive sort. But remember I said writing creatively? The next two statements may surprise you:

Example #1	Example #2
Done up the company website using HTML and Java scripting.	Initiated and hosted the company's first Asia Pacific's HOME PAGE on the Internet.

Fig. 9.2 Accomplishment & Achievement #2

Both statements are stating the same about what a programmer had done in a start-up internet company. The statement on the left is a classic example of job description using roles and responsibilities and stated explicitly the technical knowledge needed to accomplish it.

In contrast, the statement on the right uses words like "initiated" and "first Asia Pacific" to define an *Achievement* that elicit the business benefits this employee brought to the company. Is there any innovation involved? Absolutely No! But by carelessly writing your Achievement as Accomplishment, you will lose out to other candidates who did it otherwise.

It may also surprise you that not many people are able to recognize *Achievement* because many people do not consciously know they have achieved something in their life. If they do, they will quickly forget about it.

Case Study: Staff Appraisal
A team of engineers (20 members or so) was due for an annual appraisal. That year, the engineers were told to write their achievement

for the whole year and submit them via email to their immediate supervisor over a 3 day exercise. However, no information pertaining to "Achievement" was provided or how lengthy it should be.

This batch of engineers was made up of qualified professionals holding technical diploma to business degrees. Among them, one was already pursuing a part-time master program.

By the fourth day, the result was consolidated and the human resource folks were astounded:

- 30% of engineers never reverted with an achievement list. When they were prompted, we discovered that they were unable to differentiate achievement from accomplished tasks. Achievement then was a clever word for the human resource, not for the engineers.

- 20% of engineer wrote and asked:
  - What is an achievement list?

- How to write an achievement?

- The rest of the engineers wrote modestly hoping to represent "Achievements" in the best way they saw them.

The engineers' inputs were analyzed carefully. Now that you know how we defined Achievement and Accomplishment differently, the "achievements" written by these engineers were not the most appealing as our analysis reviewed. I extracted some and re-print the achievements below for our learning purpose. Some sentences were also reconstructed to hide the person's identity.

Accomplishment mistook for Achievement:
- "All reports are handled on time."
- "I have never missed any procedural steps."
- "I worked in the department for 7 years."

Achievement that lacks the "punch":
- "My customer is very happy with me."
- "The award was presented to me from my boss."

Good Working ethics mistook for Achievement:

- "I am very hard working."
- "I have not been late for work."

It is not conclusive from the findings that these engineers had written poorly. But there are important take-away:

- Engineers (or more correctly as professionals) do not necessary understand Achievement in the work place. If the terms Achievement and Accomplishment were explained before the appraisal starts, things may turn out differently.

- In contemporary corporate HR practices, particularly large companies, a high degree of annual appraisal depends on the achievements a staff can record. The staff now owns the career development and his supervisor provides the right opportunity. The staff is in the "driver seat".

This is a shift from the conventional practice whereby the immediate supervisor remembers the subordinates' achievements and accomplishments. The supervisor dictates very much the career path of his staff and not the staff themselves. The supervisor is in the "driver seat" instead.

New-age employee will take charge of their career. Before they forget their achievements and accomplishments, they write them down, in particular, they write them inside their resumes. In this manner, a person's resume gets updated quite frequently, every 6 months or lesser.

Consolidated Achievement

Keeping *Achievement* consolidated in one single section or in sub-sections and listing them by profession is an excellent practice. Figure 9.3 illustrates 2 preferential methods:

Instead of inter-twining *Accomplishment, Achievements* and others, 3 reasons to keep *Achievement* stand alone:

Resume
```
Professional Experience
    Profession #1
        Role & Responsibilities #1
        Accomplishments #1
    Profession #2
        Role & Responsibilities #2
        Accomplishments #2
Achievement in Career
    Achievement #1
    Achievement #2
```
Achievement in standalone section

Resume
```
Professional Experience
    Profession #1
        Role & Responsibilities #1
        Accomplishment #1
        Achievement #1

    Profession #2
        Role & Responsibilities #2
        Accomplishment #2
        Achievement #2
```
Achievement in sub-sections by profession

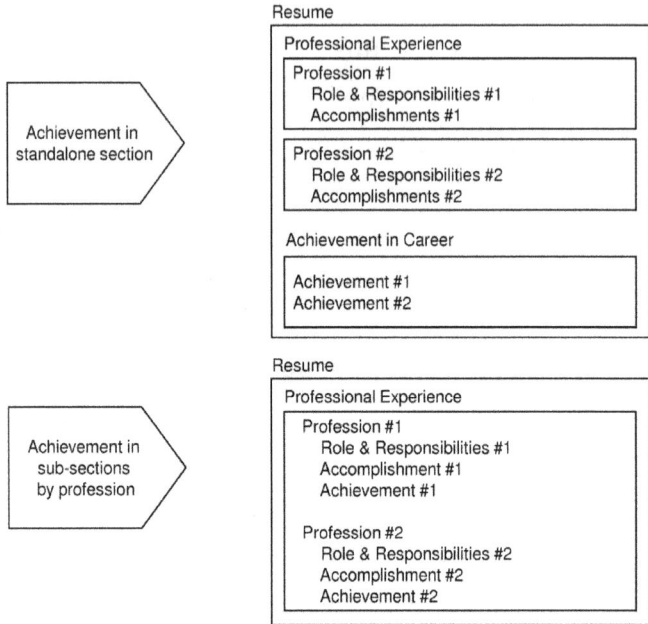

Fig 9.3 Two approaches to writing Achievement.

(a)   A consolidated paragraph is often preferred and allows the hiring manager to have quick access to the Achievements.

(b)   If the *Achievements* are scattered in a resume, you may have no written achievement in some profession without you knowing it. You may have to answer this sort of tough questions during the interview.

(c)   Finally, you get to run down your thoughts on your *Achievement.* Remember, "You know" by recalling your achievement experience. This is very different from "you think you know". And during an interview, you have no time to think it over. The run-down process becomes a preparation to help you think through without pressing the panic button in the midst of an interview.

To summarize, it is imperative to train your mind to think *Achievement* from now on.

• If you are a disciplined person, you may want to record down what you have achieved and accomplished on these basis: weekly, monthly, half yearly and so on. But in reality, not many people can do it consciously and consistently. Very quickly, the number of accomplishments and achievement can become overwhelming.

- Whenever you have to juggle between too many achievements and accomplishments, prioritize them first and pick the top 10 or at least, the top 3. Make sure they are real solid ones and you have a good story to tell why they come up on top.

- Similarly, associate the most important achievements and accomplishments for your target résumé's recipient and for the most relevant job. If you have to, break the achievements and accomplishments into different themes to bring out the best in you.

CHAPTER 10
STRATEGIES FOR WRITING "ACHIEVEMENT"

This chapter is devoted to teaching you how to write *Achievement* statement with many examples as illustration. Regular hand-on practices are the best ways to improve *Achievement* writing.

We will begin by introducing what is a factual based statement and also show you a statement structure (or syntax) which will make it fairly easy for you to get the juicy stuff written down. There is no hard or fast rule that this syntax needs be applied vigorously.

Factual Based Achievement is Superior.
A critical component of Achievement is measurability. Measurability is a quantitative metric (quantifier) that puts a unit onto the Achievement described. This unit can be in the form of number of people involved, duration or any qualitative evidence that backs the Achievement you put down.

Factual based writing style is not just restricted to writing Achievement statement. It should be a general technique used in writing compelling story lines and without the "facts", it sound loose and superfluous.

Examples of quantitative based *Achievement* statement:

- Leaded <u>7 men</u> to fix an <u>overnight</u> railroad glitch and operation resumed timely <u>the next morning</u>.
- Secured a <u>ten million deal</u> and piloted the open ceremony.

The underlined facts give more information about where, what and when and sometimes urgency of what was achieved. In instance when quantitative fact is unavailable, you will need qualitative or positive end-results to act and substantiate the achievements.

Examples of achievement supported by qualitative (non-quantitative) facts are listed below.

- Participated in the annual company marathon to <u>raise fund for National Fund Raising program</u>.
- An old lady commended me for helping her across the street. As such, I <u>won the staff model of the month.</u>

When quantitative and qualitative facts are both available, we use them generously.

- Successfully helped <u>10 toddlers</u> to improve their motors skill <u>at half the time</u> it would take using conventional method. The breakthrough was <u>recognized by the National board</u> and the method was patented.

Good Statement Syntax

A compelling Achievement statement is built from a sentence syntax containing 4 critical components:

(a) Use one <u>Action</u> word to begin your sentence and explain:

(b) <u>What</u> have you achieved?

(c) <u>Why</u> do you need to achieve it? and

(d) <u>When</u> do you achieve it?

For example, an Achievement statement may read like this: "Awarded **Certificate of Service Excellence** for Customer Satisfaction Program 2008."

	The 4 Components	Key words used
(i)	Action word	"Awarded"
(ii)	What?	"Certificate of Service Excellence"
(iii)	Why?	For the reason "Customer Satisfaction " evaluation
(iv)	When?	"2008"

Fig. 10.1 The 4 Key Components

(a)   **Begin a statement with ONE *Action* Word**

An *Action* word is a verb that carries an "actionable" motive. This will lift the energy level to begin your achievement statement. Let's do a simple experiment. Read aloud the words in Fig. 10.2. Ask yourself whether the words on the right or the left have a stronger essence.

Stronger	Weaker
Created	Worked On
Acquired	Learned
Awarded	Received
Managed	Liaised

Fig. 10.2 Strong & Weak verbs.

The words on the left column have a deliberated "power" to deliver a stronger and lasting essence. Below is another list of powerful *Action* words you can use immediately. There are endless *Action* words found in Thesauruses.

Supervised	Standardized	Piloted
Achieved	Coordinated	Leaded
Designed	Self-improved	Enhanced
Succeeded	Revised	Contributed

Fig. 10.3 More action-oriented verbs.

(b)   What have you achieved?

Most people are able to write down the "what" of an achievement but there is a difference between a good and bad statement.

The Good Achievement Statement
"Achieved close to half a million dollars of sales revenue for fiscal year 2009 within the first 6 months."

The Bad Achievement Statement
"Achieved from small to large, sales revenue was met consecutively and highest closure was recorded sometime in June 2009."

What is wrong with **The Bad** version? It gave the reader a lot of guess work, for example, ".. from small to large..." and "highest"...but at what point?

The Good version gave a summary of the achievement with quantifiable numbers, for example, "...half a million dollars...".and "within the first 6 month"

(c) **<u>Why</u> do you need to achieve it?**

You should take extra effort to explain why an achievement is remarkable and why is it important.

- A professional significance. For example, as a salesman, "for achieving this quarter's sales target"

- A professional significance with an exceptional value. For example, as a salesman, "for creating a new market campaign loved by the youth grouped between 12 to 18 years old"

- An opportunity reflecting your true values and beliefs outside your profession. For example, as a salesman, "for raising funds to help the needy through participating in annual marathon runs organized by our company".

- A good explanation also tells your prospective employer that you are accountable for the purpose of your work.

(d) <u>**When**</u> **do you achieve it?**

"When" refers to the time that the achievement was accomplished. And time can be used creatively to relay an absolute time, a relative time or a duration as illustrated below:

- Currency of accomplishment. For example, ended October 2007.

- Speed of accomplishment. For example, within the first 6 months

- "A point in time" or "An interval in time".
  For example, "in fiscal year 2007" and "from October 2007 to May 2009" etc.

Also, **When** tells the prospective employer that you are a time manager and you have good time-keeping habit.

In summary, the **For** and **When** are frequently left-out in many resumes. It is important that you should use them to harness your achievement writing.

More Examples of Achievement Statements

The following examples of achievement statements are targeting at professions and executives. These categories are not the most exhaustive. If you wish to replicate them on to your own resume, do remember to quote realistic story lines and factual based examples that you can recite clearly in the middle of an job interview.

(a)   Sales Target Achieved

- Achieved close to half a million dollars of sales revenue for fiscal year 2009 within the first 6 months.

- Won more than a half million dollars worth of contract in partnership with another <company name> division in year 2008.

(b)   Cost Reduction Effort

- Achieved over USD100,000 of cost reduction through vendor's contract optimization in fiscal year 2008.

(c)   Leadership

- Appointed as the company's work improvement leader. I coordinated the team to generate ideas. To date, 7 projects were approved by the company's management team. All projects were implemented on time with the assistance of my coordinating effort.

- Promoted from the level of junior engineer, I supervised a team of 5 technicians achieving zero defects requirements from year 2007 to 2008.

(d)   Commendation

- Achieved more than 92% of customer satisfaction rating through annual user satisfaction survey with assigned customer accounts in fiscal year 2007 to 2008.

- Awarded *Certificate of Service Excellence* for Customer Satisfaction Program 2006.
- Awarded token of appreciation in partnership with a <company name> division to deliver service operation to approx. 180 academic institutes for Ministry of Education in fiscal year 2009.

(e)   Invention & Innovation

- Received the company's highest innovation award for improved printers design and technology. The innovation was translated into production and won the company best in overall printer designed as published in "<IT> magazine" in October 2008.

- Developed data maintenance software to allow operational data to be retrieved and processed rapidly during field exercises.

(f)   First To Kick Start

- Led and implemented the first formalized professional training program for engineers in year 2008.

- Initiated and hosted the company's first Asia Pacific's HOME PAGE on the Internet.

(g)   Training & Being a Trainer

- Created the company's computing manual and conducted training for non-executive staff.

- Revised up to 70% of the latest version of in-house training documentation and conducted hands-on training for in-house staff with the revised manual.

- Designed first courseware in year 2008. Used courseware for in-house training and cordially invited by other

<company name> service group to deliver courses repeatedly.

(h) Team Player

- Won ISO 9001:2008 for excellent operation delivery and as an active ISO committee member and an internal auditor.

- Contributed actively in internet marketing for web site http:\\www.xxx.com including content enrichment, traffic creation, hits monitoring, branding and affiliated program launches.

(i) Deployment Effort

- Leaded and enhanced local business system to meet IT requirement from new computerized production plant.

- Transferred and project managed core business system into Malaysia's plant.

- Achieved a speedy deployment of 13 trade fair exhibitions including management effort for the team throughout the entire trade fair. Verbal but positive comments were received for achieving customer satisfaction.

(j) Documentation Effort

- Engineered and documented processes and operation procedures for company-wide standardization purpose.

There will be a never ending list of examples. The syntax structure is fundamentally useful in building compelling achievement statements. In addition, regular self-practices and proof-read by your friends are good ways to gain writing experience and receiving feedback.

ADDITIONAL

READINGS

CHAPTER 11
COVER LETTER

Many job applicants omit the Cover Letter totally. Especially with internet online job application, clicking a button to apply for a job was so convenient without a serious thought about cover "email". Then there is another group that uses Cover Letter so generously for mass-mailing their job application.

Let's get back to basic: the first-cut screening.

Will Cover Letter Be Screened During The First Cut?
You will be curious to know if cover letter is screened during the first-cut? "First-Cut" is a means to pick the best candidate for interview while the hiring manager goes through a chunk of resumes. And not necessary the most presentable resume is picked up.

Contrary to the popular belief that a cover letter is hardly noticed by hiring manager; I have came across hiring managers that screen cover letters during their first-cut. I asked them why? They look for job applicants that fall into one of these categories: a follower, a salesman or a marketer.

A *follower* is one who explicitly stated the purpose of the cover letter by expressing his interest in the job, telling you his current and expected salary and of course, a reminder that his or her resume is attached.

A *salesman*, include a similar follower's write out and summarized his or her career experience. He often borrowed some of achievement from his resume and high-lighted to you as his unique selling point (USP in short).

A **marketer** is one who lures you with his USP. However, he or she writes in a way to entice you to have an interview first before reading his resume.

The hiring managers admitted that because of a Marketer's USP in the cover letter, the hiring managers pay extra attention to you. Now that you get more attention, it is also the beginning of your nightmare!

The hiring manager will validate the said uniqueness against your resume. Now that the hiring manager bothers to pay attention to your resume, it means your resume has to be even clearer and concise and it has to be easier to locate your said unique selling points. If you fail to prove what you claimed, you could discount yourself in the mind of the hiring manager. Therefore, a marketer's type of resume works both ways. If you want to be a marketer, remember: don't shoot yourself.

Strategic Use of Cover Letter
Now that we understood how the cover letter is related to first-cut screening, your opening and introduction will become the "pre-resume" appetizer. In Cover Letter writing, these approaches may be used:

(a)   Up sell yourself hard enough even you have to talk on top of what was already written on the resume because you love that job so much. You will tell the hiring manager about your experiences, accomplishments and achievements centered on the desired job in the cover letter.

Some candidates don't even attach resumes with the cover letter because they are very confident that the hiring managers will invite them to send their resumes over.

(b)   Help to re-direct the reader's attention to a particular area within your resume. For example, you may provide reference to a small but important cross functional role which the reader may miss out.

(c)   Include a brief summary of your work experience most relevant to the job applied. This suggests that some job applicants have more than 1 cover letter for different job types.

Up Sell Techniques
Having spent a fair bit of time exploring crafty cover letters, 3 techniques that could up sell

you right out of your cover letter and gain you access to an interview are namely; Qualitative (Vs Quantitative Writing Technique, Benefits (Vs Features) Writing Technique and Push (Vs Pull) Writing Technique.

(a) Qualitative (Vs Quantitative technique) Writing Technique

To demonstrate the differences between salesman and marketer, we took the profile of a young manager who is relatively successful in a business development role. He made an impressive $15 million worth of sales last year in his last employment.

Salesman ←----------------→ Marketer

Make $15 million worth of sales last year	Grow the business by $5 million profit compare to last year	Grow the business by 20% every year since 2005.

Fig. 11.2 Qualitative Vs Quantitative Writing Style

Our young manager's achievement was written in 3 different cuts from a salesman to a marketer.

For a business development position, many hiring managers would agree that to make a $15 million worth of sales a year can be overstated or understated depending on the industry or the company which the new job is offered. For a less than 1 million turnover company, this applicant may not be an ideal target. However, for a company whose expected sales turnover per salesman is $10 million per year, another candidate making $20 million a year will beat our $15-million-dollar guy hands down. This is based on the assumption that we are comparing an apple for an apple.

When a company is keen to seek for an individual who can grow its business, It is not good enough to tell the hiring manager how you grew your last company with $5 million of sales revenue.

Is this what the hiring manager really looking for? To hire a business development manager, he needs an individual who has the experience to grow a business consistently, not just $5 million last year.

The writing style on the far right (see figure 11.2) withstands test and time because it not only qualifies the business development effort but it states explicitly the success rate as a percentage average (20%) over several years. The latter adds the qualitative muscles on top of quantitative achievement. It teases the reader to predict your future sales performance based on your previous achievement.

(b)   **Benefits Vs Features**

A Salesman writing style discussed in the last section is "feature" based. Imagine the salesman as an end product; the salesman will describe himself to the reader in a self-centered manner – a narration of features after features.

Some feature-based examples include:

- Achieved a $5 million of sales turn over in year 2003.
- Won the most productive staff of the month award.
- Led a team of 3 engineers to complete the project within a year.

The listed examples will be fine if they are found in the Achievement or Accomplishment sections of the resume because they establish a point in time where efforts are completed. But they are not going to give much impact in a cover letter because whatever you achieved and accomplished, the hiring manager see no transferable value in bringing them into a new position that has yet to see you in action. You have to help the hiring manager to see that transferable and repeatable skills in your cover letter i.e. you should be marketing your benefits to the hiring manager, not your features.

In contrast, a Marketer writing style feasts you on benefits after benefits. The hiring manager looks for clues that suggest a candidate whose past experience is sustainable and repeatable. The Marketer responds by allowing the hiring manager to map his worthiness for the new position by providing quality data (and quantitative if necessary).

We can convert the Salesman – Marketer table into Features Vs Benefits as shown in fig. 11.3:

Feature ←-------------------→ **Benefit**

Make $15 million worth of sales last year	Grow the business by $5 million profit compare to last year	Grow the business by 20% every year since 2005.

Fig. 11.3 Features Vs Benefits Writing Style.

A few more examples will help you to understand the differences between features and benefits:

Feature	Benefit
Won the runner up in Best Education Tutorial Curriculum in the National Education Press 1999.	Consistent updating of Education Syllabus to meet National Education standards every year.
Used the XXX Organic Growing method to replace traditional farming method.	XXX Organic Growing promote healthy eating lifestyle, reduces the harvest waiting time by at least 50% and safe for any vegetables farming.
Led a team of 3 engineers to complete the project within a year.	Superb leadership to drive the team to complete project on time and within budget every time.

Fig. 11.4 More examples of features VS benefits.

(c) **Push (Vs Pull) Technique**

The terms Push and Pull are borrowed from common technical jargons used in the computer industry. The Pull is like an uninvited sequence to give up some resources whereas Push is an invitation (at will) to obtain resources from a willing party. Find it difficult to understand? Doesn't matter! The key thing to remember is the Push writing style – a reactive action from the hiring manager to call you up for an interview.

To leave your cover letter plainly with current salary, expected salary, contact number and so forth is a Pull writing style. The reason is you are not inviting the hiring manager to call you up for an interview i.e. there is no bait at the end of the fishing rod. What if I write the covering letter in a qualitative style and it is benefit-driven? Am I working on the Push or Pull? The answer is you are working towards the Push Technique. But that is still insufficient to get the hiring manager to pick up the phone to call you.

This is where most cover letters fail to pump up to magnetic level.

The Push writing style requires you to identify key success factors inside you, in your work environment, in your profession or in the industry that the new position is targeted. You should construct your cover letter in a way that is self-adhesive to allow the hiring manager to pick up the phone to call you right away if he wants to listen to your success stories.

For example, Kim (not the real name) had spent a number of years in the customer service industry. In the extracted cover letter below, Kim used the pull technique to establish his position in the customer service arena. He went on to sell his unique selling point (USP) which is none other than the special knowledge he knew about the industry.

Kim wrote:

"Relevant to Executive Search industry, you may be interested to hear my USP and experience in the follow areas:

- Holistic Outsourcing,
- Customizing Solution,
- Value-Added Solution and
- Locking Down Customer."

Do you want to know how Kim had projected himself to design solution from a "holistic" approach?

Do you also want to know how Kim locked down his customer?

What about "Value-Added Solution"? Kim may be lying but you are interested to find out if he really lied because Kim has such a compelling USP.

Will you pick up the phone to call Kim for an interview? Yes! You do. This is what I call a "push" writing technique.

When You Are Clueless About Cover Letter

Use this: "Appreciate your effort to consider me as a serious candidate. I think I should be a good fit based on your Job Description (JD). Nevertheless, do give me an opportunity to present myself in your interview. Resume attached."

Never leave the Cover Letter empty!

CHAPTER 12
CAREER PYRAMID

A lot of professionals (or even blue collar workers) neither have a career plan nor ability to develop one. In fact, a vast majority of us may feel that our career paths are unpredictable i.e. you embrace the job that comes along your way. This can make your career movement quite difficult to convey to your prospective employers. More importantly, you will appear "lost" especially so if you switches roles and industries frequently. This can make you lose "sight" of your career goals even though in every employment, you may be progressing forward in some ways.

In the previous chapters, we discussed how Working Experience Summary can be customized to fit the job position you aim to apply. But a career plan is to allow you to set goals which you aim to achieve over a definite period of time.

When you are massaging (or aligning) working experience and industries to form a possible career plan, a good way to lay out these experiences over a time horizon is in a pictorial diagram called a Career Pyramid.

Fig 12.1 is an example of a Career Pyramid.

- As we read from the lower to the upper part of the pyramid, the candidate moved from broad base technical IT field to a supervisory role over a time horizon. This demonstrated he had gained technical knowledge and know-how before he moved on to supervisory roles.

  It is important to note that in each of the employment, the candidate used what he had attained to support the next employment.

- The vertical bar on the right shows the span of control (or leadership) for one who started off as a technical and operation engineer to a supervisory role with more reporting subordinates.

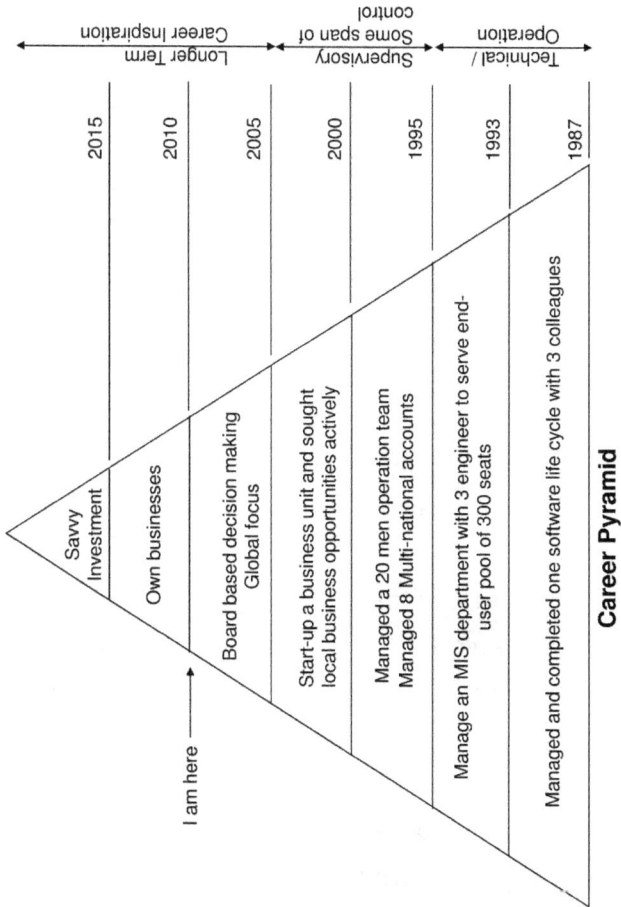

Fig 12.1 Sample of Career Pyramid

- Beyond his latest employment, the candidate expressed his wish to head for a more senior position, entrepreneurship and thereafter able to invest wisely.

Should Career Pyramid Be Shown to Hiring Manager or Distribute Freely With the Resume?

It is not necessary that the Career Pyramid you created be shown to the hiring manager. However, when you are ready to show it to a hiring manager, you are fairly confident that you are in charge of your career.

If you decide to show it to a hiring manager, I urge you to think carefully. Unlike a resume, a Career Pyramid may reveal more sensitive information about you. A Career Pyramid takes one step further to establish your long term goals, sometimes in greater details. Having identified what and how to pursue a career is good from a personal perspective but not necessary for the hiring managers. Unlike a resume, a Career Pyramid is not a marketing brochure. Do evaluate the impact before you decide to show your Career Pyramid to the public.

Shaping the Career Pyramid

The idea of a Career Pyramid is to create a mental picture of a sound, well-thought plan about your personal, career development path. It is more concrete if you could draft out that mental picture on paper and Career Pyramid is the tool.

Your creativity may shape the Career Pyramid the way you want from bottom of the pyramid to the top:

(a)   Graduates tend to land on jobs that fit closest to their field of studies. But there are many exceptions.

(b)   For people who have been changing their careers by frequent job hopping, Career Pyramid is a good starting point to look at the "pyramid" from bottom up and you decide if you want to move up or sideway.

In the process of visualizing what to "move up", you will insert the "how to" to get there. You will do the same if you decide to move sideways.

(c) For people who pursuit career to hit the millionaire dream (who does not?), a careful, thought-out Career Pyramid will serve as check points to mark your progresses and for some, to confirm accomplishments at every step.

(d) For people who experiences retrenchment, set-backs and leaving gaps between employments, you will need to cover the gaps and tracks carefully when using Career Pyramid.

What is a Gap?
Gap is the period that you are unemployed. In the gap, list down factual activities that keep you busy:

- Full – time job hunting
- Housekeeping and better bonding with your kid, something you have

missed for 10 years with your busy working life

- Help your father in his café business etc.

What is a Track?

Track is what you do that relate meaningfully back to your previous employments including:

- Attending seminar and conferences to increase awareness and networks
- Doing part time Telesales, a reverse from commanding people when you were the Sales Manager in your last job
- Freelancing (whatever)
- Mission trips to save mother Earth etc.

By covering gaps and laying out the tracks, hiring managers will think that you have kept yourself active during the retrenched period as compare to another person that does nothing at all other than applying for jobs and hoping for jobs interviews.

CHAPTER 13
FRESH OUT OF SCHOOL?
NO SWEAT!

If you are a fresh graduate without prior working experience, take the next 10 minutes to think about how you can write your own resume.

YES! I said you write your own resume.

Fresh graduates often think that they have no industry experience and therefore they cannot write a convincing resume to seek a job.

And you wrote your resume. You came up with a resume filled with your residential address, contact number, age, academic qualification and the schools you attended. Obviously, the data you just provided are plain information and the hiring managers are not likely to be interested in the statistical data. Is there a better way than this?

Sell Academic, Non-Job Achievements
Now, try to answer all of these questions below:

- What are your school's grades?

- Have you won any awards in your school?

- Which school' subjects are you specialized in and why do you think so?

- Which school's subject is closest to your career inspiration and you think you are cut for it? Why?

- What are your school projects and why did you feel proud about them?

- What are your roles in the school's volley ball team? What are your team's winnings last summer? Why do you feel so proud about the winnings even if your team has never made it to the top 3 position?

- What have you been doing consistently about your hobbies and wish to be part of you working life?

- What other languages can you speak and write? Some Europeans can actually converse well in Mandarin - an essential language to do business in China.

In a series of questions above, your answers will mould the resume into a self-marketing brochure by reciting what you have done so well back in your school days. Given a junior position, hiring managers will be keen to offer the position to fresh graduates that demonstrate sound achievement logged during the school days. Instead of focusing on your weakness i.e. industry experience that most fresh graduates fall short of, you drill down on your school days' achievements.

ABOUT THE AUTHOR

Peng Yeow has over 20 years of experience in the executive profession. He has moved from a technical to business management roles.

Candidate screening, interviewing and hiring are key deliverables in his profession. Having screened many resumes, Peng Yeow has sharpened the skill to hand-pick successful resume that ticks employer during a "first cut" screening. His practical approach to creative writing with deliberate fact-based support is superior to smart-looking, content-flabby resume.

Peng Yeow conducts resume "sharpening" workshops and provides resume cum personal portfolio writing and consultation.

Website: http://www.TitaniumCV.com.